MYSTERY EXPLORERS™

SEARCHING FOR

THE BERMUDA TRIANGLE

rosen publishing's
rosen
central®

Vivian E. Shumway
and Aaron Rosenberg

New York

Published in 2012 by The Rosen Publishing Group, Inc.
29 East 21st Street, New York, NY 10010

First Edition

Library of Congress Cataloging-in-Publication Data

Shumway, Vivian E.
Searching for the Bermuda Triangle/Vivian E. Shumway, Aaron Rosenberg.—1st ed.
    p. cm.—(Mystery explorers)
Includes bibliographical references (p.) and index.
ISBN 978-1-4488-4759-4 (library binding)—
ISBN 978-1-4488-4771-6 (pbk.)—
ISBN 978-1-4488-4779-2 (6-pack)
1. Bermuda Triangle. I. Rosenberg, Aaron. II. Title.
G558.S55 2012
001.94—dc22

                                                                2011006467

Manufactured in the United States of America

CPSIA Compliance Information: Batch #S11YA: For further information, contact Rosen Publishing, New York, New York, at 1-800-237-9932.

CONTENTS

INTRODUCTION

The Twilight Zone. The Hoodoo Sea. The Limbo of the Lost. The Devil's Triangle. The Magic Rhombus. The Port of Missing Ships. The Triangle of Death.

These are all names given to the same mysterious location, a triangular area of ocean with a long and perilous history. But most people nowadays know it by its most famous name, one that can still send a shiver through sailors and aviators—the Bermuda Triangle.

The Triangle can't be found on any standard maps. The United States Board of Geographic Names does not recognize the Bermuda Triangle as an official name, and it does not have an official file on that area. And, because it is part of a larger body of water, the Triangle does not have any specific boundaries or markers.

Usually the Triangle is described as extending from Miami, Florida, to Bermuda, to San Juan, Puerto Rico, and from there back up to Miami—roughly 500,000 square miles (1,295,000 square kilometers) of the Atlantic Ocean. Some say that it stretches even farther, as far as the coast of Virginia with one corner and the shore of Cuba or the Dominican Republic with the other. Indeed, some of the estimates for the Triangle range as high as 1,500,000 square miles (3,884,000 square km) in area.

There are two facts, however, on which everyone agrees. The first is that the Bermuda Triangle lies in the Atlantic Ocean, off the southeastern coast of the United States. The second is that it has been the site of an unusually high number of bizarre disappearances. Boats, planes, and people have all vanished

The *Star Tiger* was an Avro Tudor IV plane like the one shown here. It disappeared without a trace on January 30, 1948. Twenty-five passengers and six crew members were on board.

there without a trace. The mystery of the Bermuda Triangle has baffled people for hundreds of years. Is there a scientific explanation? Or is it truly something that cannot be explained except by the supernatural? In this book, we will explore the mystery of the Bermuda Triangle from all angles: the scientific and the supernatural.

CHAPTER 1

A Mysterious Place

The Bermuda Triangle encompasses some of the most popular tourist locations in the world. It has always seen a great deal of water traffic (and later, in the twentieth century, air traffic as well), starting with the earliest recorded account in 1492 when Columbus sailed through it to get to the New World. The Triangle's eastern point is also not that far from the birthplace of most of the Atlantic Ocean hurricanes, which form off the northwest coast of Africa, and is often home to its own type of spectacular and unpredictable storms. In fact, a single storm in the region of the Triangle can produce as much as 10 inches (25 centimeters) of rain in just a matter of hours. The Gulf Stream runs through the Triangle, altering the water currents in that area, and beneath the Triangle's surface lie some of the Atlantic's deepest waters—as much as 30,000 feet (9,144 meters) deep! Just to add to the watery confusion, scientists recently discovered an ocean current running hundreds of feet beneath the Gulf Stream—but going in the opposite direction!

Also known as the Devil's Triangle, the Bermuda Triangle is a small part of the Atlantic Ocean allegedly responsible for several disappearances of ships and aircraft.

Gian Quasar

If one person can be called the "leading expert" on the Bermuda Triangle phenomenon, it's Gian Quasar. He has compiled over 350 cases of Bermuda Triangle disappearances and strange occurrences from the last two centuries, publishing books on the subject and even starting a Web site documenting the latest Bermuda Triangle news. He has also documented other mysteries, like Bigfoot and the Loch Ness Monster.

And there's yet another oddity to the Bermuda Triangle. Usually, at least in the rest of the world, there are two measurements of north. The first is called magnetic north. This is the direction seen on a compass. The second is called true north. This is the actual geographic direction. Normally, the two measurements of north are off by as much as 20 degrees. This is known as compass variation, and compasses have to be adjusted to account for the difference. But the Bermuda Triangle is one of only two spots on the planet where magnetic north and true north are perfectly aligned.

There's another strange area not too far from the Bermuda Triangle. This is called the Sargasso Sea after its floating, tangled jungles of sargassum seaweed. The Sargasso Sea lies east of Bermuda and south of the Gulf Stream, in the middle of the Atlantic. It does overlap the Bermuda Triangle at its northwestern edge and the Triangle's easternmost side, but the Sargasso is over 2,000,000 square miles (5,180,000 square km) of ocean, four times the generally accepted

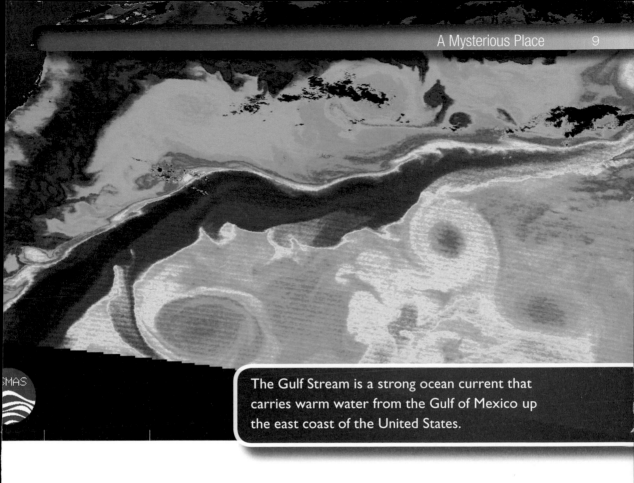

The Gulf Stream is a strong ocean current that carries warm water from the Gulf of Mexico up the east coast of the United States.

size of the Triangle. Despite this, the Bermuda Triangle is often linked to the Sargasso Sea, and at times the two are even considered one and the same, and they are often featured in the same tales. Part of this confusion is probably due to the Sargasso's own oddity—in addition to its seaweed jungle, its waters are warm and constantly swirl clockwise, despite a lack of wind.

Actually, very few facts are known about the Bermuda Triangle. This only serves to increase everyone's interest, of course. Unsolved mysteries always attract attention—particularly when there may be undisclosed secrets as well.

CHAPTER 2

Origins of the Legend

Early sea explorers wrote in their journals of strange occurrences, bizarre events that seemed to make no sense. Many of these events took place in or near the Sargasso Sea—and the Bermuda Triangle.

The first recorded incident in the Bermuda Triangle was written by one of the most famous sailors of all time—Christopher Columbus. In 1492, Columbus was on his famous journey, which would eventually lead him to the West Indies. He noted that the ship's compass was acting strangely and giving inaccurate readings, and at one point he saw a great ball of fire shoot across the sky and crash into the sea. Columbus was under a great deal of pressure at the time. His crew had begun to panic because there was no land in sight and the ship had only a certain amount of food and water—and some of that had to be saved for the journey home. The last thing that

Christopher Columbus reported some of the first strange phenomena in the Bermuda Triangle during one of his voyages to the West Indies.

Columbus would have wanted to do was to point out weird readings or fireballs to his crew.

But there were other witnesses. On October 11, Columbus and one of his crew both saw a light over the water, one that vanished quickly. Only hours later, the crew spotted land: the islands of the West Indies. While none of his three ships disappeared or crashed, the records of his bizarre sightings did add to notions that the waters in that area were not exactly ordinary and possibly even dangerous.

And then the recorded disappearances began.

Disappearing Ships

In 1609, a sailing ship called the *Sea Venture* disappeared right off the coast of Bermuda. A rescue boat was sent after it, but that one vanished as well. These are the earliest known disappearances in the Bermuda Triangle, but they were only the beginning.

A little over a hundred years went by without any major problems. But then, in 1750, three Spanish galleons accompanying the *Nuestra Señora de Guadalupe* disappeared off the coast of North Carolina.

It wasn't until the nineteenth century that the disappearances began happening in earnest. Sixty-two years after the Spanish galleons vanished, in 1812, the *Patriot*, an American packet ship, disappeared in the Gulf Stream. This caused a great deal of excitement because the missing ship was carrying Vice President Aaron Burr's daughter, Theodosia. Neither the *Patriot* nor any of its passengers were ever heard from again.

The *Mary Celeste* is one of the most famous vessels to tangle with the Bermuda Triangle. When the ship was recovered off the coast of Portugal, there was no one on board.

Two years later, in 1814, the U. S. warship *Wasp* vanished off the coast of South Carolina.

But the next incident to capture people's attention and imagination was not a disappearance but a weird reappearance. In 1840, the French vessel the *Rosalie* was found drifting in the Triangle. Her sails were set and she was undamaged, but she was utterly unmanned. Her cargo was untouched. Clearly she hadn't been set upon by pirates. With no sign of damage, it makes no sense to think that some emergency forced an evacuation. No trace of her passengers or crew was ever found.

The *Mary Celeste*

The *Rosalie* was not the most famous unmanned ship, however. That honor goes to another of the great names in sailing history—the *Mary Celeste*. On November 5, 1872, the *Mary Celeste* left New York Harbor and headed for Genoa. It was carrying a cargo of industrial alcohol, the type used for medicinal and other purposes than drinking. Captain Benjamin Spooner Briggs was in control of the vessel. Also on board were his wife, his two-year-old daughter, and eight crewmen. On December 5, 1872, the *Dei Gratia* found the *Mary Celeste* floating in the Atlantic Ocean. One lifeboat was missing, as were the people, but otherwise the ship was intact and everything was properly stowed, including personal belongings. Whatever had driven the captain, his family, and his crew to leave had apparently forced them to move quickly. The last position recorded in the *Mary Celeste*'s log put her

The *Maria Celestia*

Some historians speculate that some of the confusion regarding the connection between the Bermuda Triangle and the famed mystery of the *Mary Celeste* was caused by simple name confusion. In 1864, a Civil War blockade runner, the *Maria Celestia* (sometimes known as the *Mary Celestia* or the *Marie Celeste*), sank after she struck a reef off of Bermuda's South Shore—eight years before the *Mary Celeste* was discovered abandoned off the coast of Portugal. Over time the stories began to overlap, and now many people have come to regard them as one and the same, even though there was only one casualty during the sinking of the *Maria Celestia*. Today, tourists can dive down and see the *Maria Celestia*, which lies under about 55 feet (17 m) of water off the coast of Bermuda. Her paddlewheels, boilers, and anchor are all still intact.

roughly 100 miles (160 km) west of the Azores, which meant she would have passed near or through the Bermuda Triangle—almost 400 miles (644 km) off course. Of course, there are some who claim that the *Mary Celeste* was never in the Triangle and that her fate had nothing mysterious about it—that the Triangle element was added later, after the Triangle had caught everyone's attention. But that doesn't solve the mystery of what happened to the captain and crew.

The fact remains that the mystery of the fate of the captain and crew of the *Mary Celeste* has never been solved. There have been many theories—some very compelling—but the mystery remains.

CHAPTER 3

The Legend and the Pop Culture Icon

W here does the name "Bermuda Triangle" come from?

Surprisingly, even though that area of the Atlantic has featured heavily in folktales and legends—as well as in the horror stories of sailors—for centuries, the Bermuda Triangle's name isn't even a century old. In fact, it wasn't until the twentieth century that the public began to hear of it. In 1950, a reporter named E. V. W. Jones mentioned the area in an Associated Press dispatch— he talked about the mysterious disappearances of ships and planes between Bermuda and the Florida coast. That got the public's attention!

Two years later, another reporter, George X. Sand, wrote an article for *Fate* magazine, talking about a "series of strange marine disappearances, each leaving no trace whatever, that have taken place in the past few years" in a "watery triangle bounded roughly by Florida, Bermuda and Puerto Rico."

JUNE

25 CENTS
IN CANADA 30 CENTS

AMAZING STORIES

Amazing Stories, a science fiction magazine launched in 1926, had its own theories for the mysterious disappearances in the Bermuda Triangle.

Scientifiction Stories by

A. Hyatt Verrill
John W. Campbell, Jr.
Edmond Hamilton

Now the public was really interested. Soon others began writing about the area as well. M. K. Jessup, in his book *The Case for the UFO*, claimed that the disappearances were actually alien abductions. Donald E. Kyhoe said much the same in his 1955 book, *The Flying Saucer Conspiracy*. The Triangle began to appear in science fiction stories, particularly with this idea of alien involvement.

Then, in February 1964, a writer named Vincent Gaddis wrote a piece for the magazine *Argosy*, in which he discussed "the Deadly Bermuda Triangle" and what a large number of disappearances the area had seen— or perhaps had caused. Gaddis later expanded the article into a book, called *Invisible Horizons: True Mysteries of the Sea*. The *Argosy* editors were delighted with the article and the readers' enthusiastic response and ran more details and follow-ups. A letter in their May 1964 issue talked about a plane that had flown over the area in 1944 and never returned. In August 1968, *Argosy*'s cover story was "The Spreading Mystery of the Bermuda Triangle."

The Triangle's Popularity Expands

The Triangle now not only had its name, it had caught public interest, and it continued to do so. In 1969, John Wallace Spencer wrote a book called *Limbo of the Lost*, which was specifically about the Triangle. But what really established the Bermuda Triangle as a phenomenon was the feature documentary *The Devil's Triangle*, which was released in 1971, and a book called *The Bermuda*

The Devil's Sea

When you've finished reading this book, maybe you'll think, "I am never traveling through the Bermuda Triangle if I can help it!" Not so fast! Did you know that there are other places around the globe that are linked to several mysterious disappearances as well? The most famous of these is the Devil's Sea (also known as the Dragon's Triangle). Like the Bermuda Triangle, the Devil's Sea is not located on any map, but if you do any traveling off the coast of Japan, you may very well run into it.

According to the book *The Dragon's Triangle* by Charles Berlitz, from the years of 1952 to 1954, five Japanese military vessels vanished, along with their crews—a total of over seven hundred people! The Japanese government, seeing that the area was apparently dangerous, sent out a team of one hundred scientists to investigate. Their vessel also disappeared. Later reports showed that Berlitz's account of some of the events was exaggerated, but the mystery of the Devil's Sea remains.

Triangle, which was written by Charles Berlitz and published in 1974. Berlitz has been accused of manipulating his readers, of never offering any concrete answers, and of deliberately exaggerating and even fabricating details. But no matter what critics said, *The Bermuda Triangle* quickly became a best seller, and soon almost everyone was talking about the Bermuda Triangle and its dangerous or maybe even supernatural nature.

After *The Bermuda Triangle*, Berlitz continued to excite readers with books about the Roswell Incident, Atlantis, the search for Noah's Ark, the Philadelphia Experiment, and the Dragon's Triangle. He passed away in 2003 at the age of eighty-nine.

CHAPTER 4

The Famous Bermuda Triangle

With the rising popularity of the Bermuda Triangle mystery, it was no surprise that several movies, television specials, and books grew out of it.

Vanished!

During the 1980s and early 1990s, children and teens were given the chance to decide how a story would unfold with the Choose Your Own Adventure series of books. The series has sold over 250 million copies, including the popular title *Vanished!* from 1986, which gives readers a chance to face the Bermuda Triangle head-on as they venture into it in search of a missing friend. One wrong turn could get you abducted by aliens, eaten by a giant squid, or attacked by ghost pirates.

The Bermuda Triangle has remained the focus of many books for teens and

DAVID COPPERFIELD AND THE BERMUDA TRIANGLE

Illusionist David Copperfield was always looking for the next great illusion during the height of his television popularity in the 1980s. Famous for making things like the Statue of Liberty and the Orient Express disappear, Copperfield met his match in a 1988 television special when he made himself disappear—into the Bermuda Triangle. In the dramatic final scene, Copperfield reappears just in time to see the boat he was riding on explode into flames, apparently because of the effects of the Triangle. But like any good illusionist, he escaped unscathed in a dramatic helicopter rescue. Copperfield has won twenty-one Emmy Awards for his television specials.

children, most recently with the Devil's Triangle series written and illustrated by B. C. Hailes.

The Bermuda Triangle on the Big Screen

The Bermuda Triangle has also been the focus of several movies and TV shows, mostly making appearances in B-movie features, such as 1979's *Mystery*

David Copperfield helped to fuel the pop culture infamy of the Bermuda Triangle during the 1980s with his television special. Copperfield disappeared into the Triangle and miraculously returned.

in the Bermuda Triangle (Misterio en las Bermudas), starring Mexican professional wrestlers Santo and Blue Demon.

In 2001's television movie *The Triangle*, starring Luke Perry and Dan Cortese, a group of friends sail out in search of riches and find themselves trapped and lost in the Bermuda Triangle.

Horror feature *Triangle*, released in 2009, has been compared to *Memento* and *The Machinist* with its nonstandard plot twists. Despite being generally panned by critics, the film has developed a cult following among horror fans.

A Great Bermuda Triangle Movie?

In 2010, rumors began to fly about a possible Indiana Jones finale that would send Indiana Jones, played by Harrison Ford, to investigate the mysteries surrounding the Bermuda Triangle. The rumors proved to be false, but this shows that the movie-going public is hungry for more feature films about the Bermuda Triangle.

CHAPTER 5

The Bermuda Triangle in the Twentieth Century

The Bermuda Triangle did not become any less dangerous in the twentieth century—far from it. As more and more ships crossed the Atlantic every year, more and more ships disappeared into the Triangle never to be seen again. The Triangle doesn't seem to care about nationality, either—ships from all over the world have been its victims.

In 1902, the German vessel *Freya* was found in the region of the Triangle. It was listing badly to one side, part of its mast was gone, and its crew had vanished.

In March 1918, the USS *Cyclops*, captained by the eccentric Lieutenant Commander George W. Worley, left Barbados for Baltimore. Days later, with the ship long overdue, a massive search was launched. But no trace of the *Cyclops* was ever found. It was the largest ship in the navy, and it had left Barbados with three hundred people on board.

The USS *Cyclops* had been in Brazil to help refuel British ships. While on her way back, the ship was last seen near Barbados.

In 1924 the Japanese freighter *Raifucu Maru* radioed for help—but the ship and its crew were never found.

In 1941, the USS *Cyclop*'s two sister ships, *Proteus* and *Nereus*, both vanished while traveling from the Virgin Islands to the United States—one month apart.

In 1945, five torpedo bombers along with their crew members disappeared around the Bermuda Triangle, along with the thirteen crew members of the Mariner, which was sent to look for them.

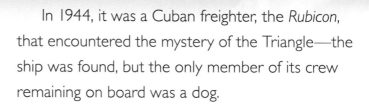

In 1944, it was a Cuban freighter, the *Rubicon*, that encountered the mystery of the Triangle—the ship was found, but the only member of its crew remaining on board was a dog.

Airplanes Join the Mystery

As the airplane became more common toward the middle of the twentieth century and both passenger and cargo flights began to cross Atlantic waters, the Triangle began claiming airplanes as well as ships as its prey.

In 1945, the most famous of all the Bermuda Triangle disappearances took place. This was the mystery of Flight 19.

It began without any unusual incidents. On December 5, 1945, Flight 19 left the Fort Lauderdale air base on a routine training mission. Lieutenant Charles Taylor, an experienced pilot and instructor, was patrol leader. He was flying a navy Avenger bomber. Four other Avengers flew with him, each one under the control of a rookie pilot. The training mission itself, a test bombing run followed by several turns, was a complete success.

THE *STAR TIGER*: MYSTERY SOLVED?

According to a 2009 story by the BBC, the mystery of the disappearance of the *Star Tiger* may have been solved.

Commercial flights from London to Bermuda were fraught with peril in the 1940s. They required a stop to refuel along the way because the flight was over 2,000 miles (3,219 km) long. And British South American Airways, which operated the route, had a terrible safety record, resulting in eleven accidents and five lost planes over the course of three years. And a closer look at the accident report holds a number of interesting clues. The heater on the *Star Tiger* was unreliable and had failed before the disappearance. One of the compasses on the plane was also found to be malfunctioning. Experts suggest that in order to keep the plane warmer, the pilot decided to fly at a lower altitude, which burns fuel faster. On its approach to Bermuda, the *Star Tiger* was likely slightly off course and running low on fuel. Also, flying at only 2,000 feet (610 m) above sea level, there would be no room for sudden emergency maneuvers. According to a BBC interview with Eric Newton, a Ministry of Civil Aviation air accident investigator, "At 2,000 feet, you'd be leaving very little altitude for maneuver. In any serious in-flight emergency they could have lost their height in seconds and gone into the sea," leaving no time to send an emergency signal. So, whether an emergency occurred or the plane simply ran out of fuel, it seems that the mystery of the *Star Tiger* might at last be solved.

But on the return flight, Taylor began to have some strange difficulties. He radioed the base and informed them that his compass was no longer working properly and that he was confused as to the flight's current location and direction. He attempted to navigate by using landmarks, but night was falling and visibility dropped rapidly.

Then the weather worsened, as a storm set in. Fort Lauderdale was still in contact with Taylor, but the storm made communication difficult. Taylor informed the base that he was over the Gulf of Mexico and turned Flight 19 east to search for land. Unfortunately, he was probably mistaken and in fact turned away from land and back out over the Atlantic. The Avengers had only six hours worth of fuel, and as the night deepened, the navy grew more and more concerned. Finally they dispatched several planes to search for the missing flight, including a Martin Mariner. The Mariner had an enormous gas tank and could fly for twelve hours without refueling. It was the perfect plane for a long search.

But the Mariner never returned. Neither did Flight 19.

Critics claim that it wasn't so unusual for planes to have difficulties. They point out that four of the five Avengers were piloted by rookies. They also

Lost in 1945 off the coast of Fort Lauderdale, Florida, the Avenger aircrafts that were part of Flight 19 were finally located by the *Deep Sea* salvage crew in 1991.

claim that Taylor was already confused that day and simply got disoriented. But no one can explain definitively what happened to the planes—or the pilots. Each Avenger had a three-man life raft and only two men for crew. But no life rafts were ever found. Nor were there any other traces of the

Avengers or their crew—until 1991 with a discovery by the crew of the *Deep Sea*, a salvage vessel. But no one has been able to explain how they ended up at the bottom of the ocean.

The mystery of Flight 19, more than any other event, drew attention to the Bermuda Triangle. The story ran in all the papers, and soon everyone was talking about the Triangle and its appetite for ships and planes.

The mystery of the Bermuda Triangle increased in 1948. The airplane *Star Tiger* disappeared en route to Bermuda, only moments after radioing ground crew that it would arrive on schedule. A year later, the *Star Tiger*'s sister plane, the *Star Ariel*, also disappeared while traveling from Bermuda to Jamaica. Needless to say, this new pair of disappearances added to the Bermuda Triangle's fame—or maybe that should be infamy.

CHAPTER 6

Some Answers to the Mystery?

As happens with any bizarre situation, people want to find a comforting answer to the mystery. They have offered many different theories about the Bermuda Triangle and its various disappearances. Many of the theories come from scientists and are based on facts. Other theories are more imaginative.

Simple Human Error

The most commonly mentioned theory is simply that the disappearances are caused by simple human error. After all, the Bermuda Triangle includes such popular places as Miami and Bermuda. Many of the people who travel through the area are on vacation. They may be partying, maybe even drinking, or simply not really paying attention to

Mistakes fueled by alcohol and carelessness could explain some of the mysterious disappearances off the Florida coast. Miami (shown here) is a popular destination for partiers.

what they're doing. They sometimes take trips in boats that were never meant to handle ocean currents or go sailing late at night without proper lighting, without maps, and without any experience in or knowledge of the area. Such careless pleasure-seekers often find something far more dangerous than a little late-night fun—they find death on the high seas.

Exaggeration of Stories

Some skeptical people say the answer to the Bermuda Triangle's string of bizarre disappearances is that they weren't so bizarre at that or as common as they seem. These skeptics claim that the mystery is nothing but exaggeration and fabrication, whether deliberate or simply enthusiastic.

In 1975, an Arizona librarian named Larry Kusche decided to investigate the claims about the Bermuda Triangle. He published his findings in a book called *The Bermuda Triangle Mystery Solved*. In it, Kusche claimed that many of the strange accidents in the Triangle were exaggerated. He stated that ships that had vanished in calm waters actually went down in raging storms, that boats that had vanished without a trace had, in fact, been recovered, and that ships that had supposedly drowned in the Triangle had, in fact, never been anywhere near it.

In the same year, the editor of *Fate* magazine checked with the famous British insurance company Lloyd's of London, looking over accident reports from oceans around the world. What the editor found was that the Bermuda Triangle's accident rate was no higher than anywhere else. The United States Coast Guard confirms this, saying that it has never been impressed by claims of the Triangle's danger or its supernatural nature.

Compass Malfunction or Variation

The Bermuda Triangle is a dangerous place for navigators, even without any supernatural menace. Part of that is its odd lack of compass variation.

Normally a navigator has to consider the difference between the compass's north and true north, or else he could wind up guiding a boat or plane off course. In the Bermuda Triangle, where compass north and true north actually match, navigators have to remember not to compensate. If they automatically compensate for a variation that does not exist, they will wind up off course. In the middle of the ocean, such a miscalculation can be fatal.

The Effect of the Gulf Stream

Another major factor to be considered in the mystery of the Bermuda Triangle is the Gulf Stream. This current flows steadily northeast, from the tip of Florida up the Eastern Seaboard and then across the Atlantic to the United Kingdom. It divides the cold Atlantic waters from the warm Sargasso Sea, and accounts for the fog in London, as well as the more moderate temperatures in most of Europe. Thanks to the warmth of the Gulf Stream, parts of Britain that are on the same latitude as New England and Canada can grow even tropical plants like palm trees.

The Gulf Stream is not only warm and steady, it is very fast and very turbulent. An inexperienced pilot could easily lose control to it and be carried off course, winding up north and east of the right destination. The speed of the Gulf Stream could also quickly wash away any debris, explaining why ships and planes have vanished without a trace—debris caught in the Gulf Stream has wound up as far away as the North Atlantic.

Hurricanes and other types of weather could account for some disappearances into the Bermuda Triangle. Out in the middle of the ocean, sailors may not know the severity of a storm until it is upon them.

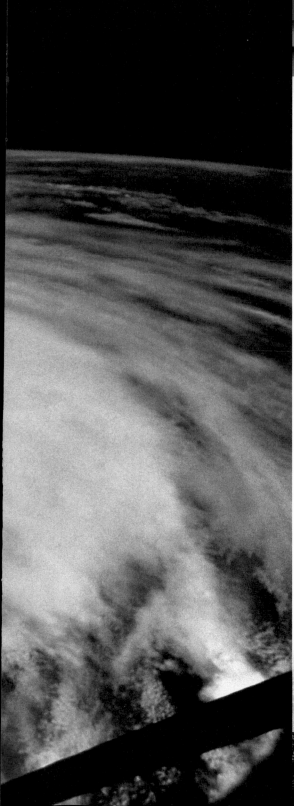

The Weather

Weather, some people say, could also be a major factor in the mystery of the Bermuda Triangle. In the Triangle, severe storms can form without warning and dissipate completely before ever reaching shore. These storms are often too small and swiftly forming for meteorologists to predict them accurately. Known as meso-meteorological storms, they can include tornadoes, thunderstorms, and tropical cyclones.

In severe weather, visibility can drop drastically, so fast that planes can literally dive into the ocean without the pilots realizing what's happening. Giant waves can be stirred up by the storms, large enough to engulf a ship and drag it under. The electricity generated by thunderstorms can short out communications and guidance systems, leaving ships and planes powerless and blind. A ship or plane

The sextant is one of the navigational tools used by sailors to measure the angle between two visible objects. But tools are worthless if a sailor is disoriented by a mysterious force.

might disappear in such a storm—and then, moments later, the storm might pass, leaving nothing but calm waters behind.

Earthquakes

One interesting theory is that the Bermuda Triangle is subject to earthquakes. Even though they would take place on the ocean floor, miles below the surface, the resulting vibrations could affect water currents up above, generating sudden waves and even whirlpools. Without sophisticated equipment to detect seismic activity—and equipment specially designed to penetrate to the ocean floor—ships could easily be swamped by the sudden shifts in pressure and wave activity.

Even without earthquakes, whirlpools can be deadly to ships. Whirlpools are created by conflicting currents in the water and can appear out of nowhere. A strong whirlpool can pull in a medium-sized ship and suck it under the water in hours or less. Lifeboats would also be pulled under, of course, limiting the possibility of survivors. Or witnesses.

Disorientation

Many of the Bermuda Triangle stories include mentions that the pilot can't see anything, reports clear weather conditions, or simply says that things look strange. This may, in fact, be the result of spatial disorientation, a very real danger often mentioned by the Federal Aviation Administration (the FAA).

Our sense of balance comes from the position of fluid and tiny hairs in our inner ears. Apparently, that inner ear fluid is affected by new changes but not

Scylla and Charybdis

Long before there were scientific explanations for strange phenomenon, sailors created their own. In the *Odyssey*, Homer describes a treacherous strait guarded on each side by one of two deadly creatures: Scylla, a many-headed monster known to drag sailors from a ship's deck and swallow them whole, and Charybdis, a deadly whirlpool known to suck entire ships down into her depths.

But the legend of these creatures has been tied to a real location, the Strait of Messina, off the coast of Italy. The strait connects the Tyrrhenian Sea and the Ionian Sea, and it is extremely treacherous because it is fairly narrow and shallow and has strong currents and whirlpools—not to mention dangerous rocks, which the locals have dubbed "Scylla."

Was the Strait of Messina the Bermuda Triangle of ancient times?

by a steady and continual change. If you tilt your head sharply to one side, you will notice a shift in your sense of balance. But if you slowly tilt your head to one side and hold it that way, the shift will be less sudden, and eventually you will not have any difficulty holding your head to the side while keeping your balance.

This is what can happen to pilots. If a plane goes into a sudden dive, the pilot would know he was diving. But if he continued to dive, after a minute his inner ear would compensate, and he would feel, wrongly, as if he'd leveled off again.

Normally, this is not a problem for pilots: they have instruments to tell them altitude and angle, and during a clear day, they can always use visual cues as well. But at night, over the ocean, there is little to see and almost no visual cues. The dark sky often blends into the dark water, so much so that you cannot tell where your horizon is. If you have lost your instruments, or are flying without instruments—or if you don't believe what your instruments are telling you—you could be flying right into the ocean without even realizing it. And the Bermuda Triangle not only doesn't offer many visual cues, its frequent storms can completely block visibility, forcing a pilot to rely on any working instruments and on "gut feeling." And as shown above, "gut feeling" isn't reliable when the inner ear is confused.

Alcohol also throws off the sense of balance, as well as the sense of judgment. As can be the case with those who have gone partying on boats when they've had too much to drink, any pilot flying over the ocean under the influence of alcohol stands a good chance of wandering into the Triangle and never returning.

Methane

One of the more unusual scientific theories concerning the Bermuda Triangle has to do with bubbles of gas. The theory states that pockets of methane gas are released from the ocean floor. Methane causes the water in that area to become less dense. This means that buoyancy there drops suddenly. If a boat were directly over a large amount of methane, the boat would lose its buoyancy and sink quickly.

This is not as bizarre as it might sound. Scientists say the Bermuda Triangle is high in natural methane hydrates. This means that released bubbles of methane gas could occur at any time, and any ship caught by enough of them could, indeed, find itself quickly sinking to the ocean floor.

CHAPTER 7
An Unsolved Mystery

Can the mystery of the Bermuda Triangle be so easily explained away as being sudden storms or mere coincidence? Some people don't think that's possible. After all, scientists have been arguing over the area for decades, yet no one theory has ever been proved, let alone generally accepted.

This is not so surprising. After all, not everything in life can be proved. Or explained. But people continue to try. The Bermuda Triangle has for centuries been a magnet for the imagination, and people other than scientists have suggested a wide variety of reasons for the area's effect on boats and planes. Some of these use bits of science or logic, but many rely upon bizarre situations that we cannot prove—or disprove. Could they be right? Anything is possible.

Alien Abduction

Did aliens abduct those missing ships and planes? Stories of alien sightings, and

Are UFOs or alien life to blame for the mysteries surrounding the Bermuda Triangle? Some people think so. Could there be some truth to their theories?

of abductions of unfortunate humans, have been recorded for centuries—as have Triangle disappearances. Abductions seem to take place in isolated areas—such as the middle of the Atlantic Ocean. Many UFO sightings and abductions involve bizarre power failures—several of the vanished planes and boats, including Flight 19, reported equipment failure. Could aliens have targeted the Triangle as a likely collection area, and made off with ships and boats—and their passengers—over the centuries? It would explain how they vanished without a trace.

Or perhaps UFOs are the cause, but not a deliberate one. After all, not every alien encounter ends in abduction and experimentation. What if a UFO had crashed into the Bermuda Triangle at some point? After all, scientists say the area is dangerous to flying ships. A UFO would presumably have advanced technology, probably run on some alternate power source we haven't figured out yet. It could still work even after such a crash, even if the crew themselves were killed. If the alien vessel were set up to automatically block signals within range, to avoid detection, that technology might still be operational. This would mean ships passing nearby and planes flying overhead would suddenly lose power and/or navigation, and would crash before they could find a way around the problem.

Or what if the aliens have landed? They would need a base of operations, and why assume they've set one up on land? If their ship can handle outer space, surely it can also function underwater. Perhaps their base is in the Atlantic Ocean, between Miami, Bermuda, and Puerto Rico—which would place it at the heart of the Triangle. Most people put up a fence around their home for privacy. Perhaps the aliens have done the same: not a physical fence

The Philadelphia Naval Yard supposedly held the top secret Philadelphia Experiment, which tested the effects of a strong magnetic field on a ship.

but some sort of energy field that knocks out any electronics in the immediate area to prevent people from scanning for and locating them.

A Top-Secret Experiment

What if humanity is to blame for the Bermuda Triangle? Often we meddle with things we don't really understand; scientists, many people believe, are particularly guilty of this fault. Such experimenting can lead to tremendous breakthroughs, but it can also lead to disasters.

In 1943, the Philadelphia Naval Yard was supposedly home to a secret experiment. American scientists were testing the effects of a strong magnetic field on a ship, using powerful generators to create an intense field around the vessel. Their goal was apparently to render the ship invisible, but the results were very different. The ship, and all its crew, disappeared. They were later reported in Norfolk, Virginia, but they vanished there as well. What if the Philadelphia Experiment succeeded, but not in creating invisibility? What if, instead, it created some sort of gateway through time and space? Any ships or planes that accidentally passed through that portal would find themselves transported into the past or the future. That would explain why we've never found remains of them. Either the wrecks have fallen apart from thousands of years of erosion, or we haven't caught up to them yet. And since the portal runs through time as well as space, it could have caused all those disappearances over the centuries. The gateway might exist throughout time, and those ships were also pulled either farther into the past or somewhere into our future!

This is only an artist's rendering of the lost city of Atlantis; photographic evidence of Atlantis would be priceless. Is the Bermuda Triangle part of the Atlantis mystery?

Even if the experiment was a failure, it might still explain the Triangle. Powerful magnets were involved. What if they created an area of magnetic instability, where magnetism goes haywire? Every electronic device flying or sailing through it could be affected. And if the area is unstable, it might fluctuate, which would explain why some ships and planes aren't affected (they passed by when the field was weaker, so it didn't interfere with them). The Bermuda Triangle does have an unusual magnetic field; it might be stranger than scientists admit. Of course, the navy denies the Philadelphia Experiment altogether—but they could simply be covering up the truth.

Lost City

Perhaps the answer lies not in modern failures but in an ancient success. The lost city of Atlantis is supposedly sunken thousands of feet below the water's

A STRANGE WEATHER PHENOMENON

What if bizarre weather was to blame for the Bermuda Triangle? A psychic named Ed Snedeker claimed that the Bermuda Triangle was caused by twisters. According to him, these twisting tunnels, like tornado funnels, exist all around us, but that they're invisible to the naked eye. These funnels move from north to south through the Bermuda Triangle, sucking up aircraft, ships, and people and carrying them off, depositing them finally at some hidden location in the Atlantic. Weather patterns are unpredictable, and the Triangle is well known to be the site of fabulous storms appearing out of nowhere. Could these funnels exist, and have those missing ships and planes been unlucky enough to be in their path? If so, somewhere there is a resting place for all those vessels. If we can ever predict the movement of those funnels, we might be able to find them all at once.

surface, but no one is sure exactly where. What if its final resting place lies within the Bermuda Triangle? Stories of Atlantis say that it was extremely advanced for its time and had technologies we still have not mastered. Many of the people who have studied the Atlantis tales think that the Atlanteans used some sort of crystals, somehow harnessing their energies. Some crystals are extremely tough and can resist a tremendous amount of damage; they could have survived the city's destruction and still be intact at the bottom of the ocean. But what if centuries of immersion in seawater have altered the structure of the crystals so that they now broadcast energies that interfere with the instruments and engines of passing boats and planes? If this is true, two of mankind's most powerful mysteries are actually one and the same, and the Bermuda Triangle is a signpost leading to Atlantis itself. Weird columns do lie in the water off Bermuda, and though scientists claim that these are per-fectly natural geological structures, there are those who state that they are part of the lost city.

Nature's Stargates

Dr. Michael Preisinger, a German historian and scuba diver, has proposed another possibility, one that might actually explain Ed Snedeker's claims (see sidebar on previous page). Preisinger believes the Bermuda Triangle is the site of naturally occurring wormholes, miniature black holes that essentially tun-nel through space. These wormholes appear and disappear at random, but they cause magnetic anomalies and their gravitational pull (similar to that of a full-sized black hole) would be strong enough to absorb any ships or planes in the vicinity, crushing them to microscopic size as they passed through the hole's event horizon. Water and air would also be pulled in, and scientists have recently learned that some black holes spin—if the wormholes did the same, they could create funnels, eerily close to Snedeker's invisible tunnels. Have science and psychic hit upon the right answer from opposite directions?

Damnation Alley

Perhaps the Bermuda Triangle is truly otherwordly—but in a supernatural sense rather than an extraterrestrial one. After all, it is also known as the Devil's Triangle. What if, as some people believe, the Bible is literally true? In that case, good and evil are real, as are heaven and hell—and you need to do good deeds to go to heaven.

But if you want to reach hell, you may only need to sail or fly over the Atlantic between Florida and Bermuda. Those who have been lost in the Bermuda Triangle may have passed through the gates of hell and are now damned for all eternity, poor lost souls who were simply in the wrong place at the wrong time.

Or perhaps the Triangle is more than a gateway—perhaps it is hell itself, and those lost souls are still trapped in there somewhere where we cannot see them, caught in eternal agony. Not everyone who passes through the Devil's Triangle disappears, of course, but perhaps those who did had committed sins and thus were damned—or perhaps this is a way to make mankind doubt and fear. Both techniques would work to the devil's advantage.

Privacy Screen

Perhaps some of these theories are partially right—the Triangle is a privacy screen, like a fence. But it's made by humanity, not by aliens. Various world governments have secret projects, things they don't want anyone else to see. What if one or more of these governments built a device to generate an electrical field around the Triangle in order to hide their activities? Even if the field doesn't stop every ship, it makes travelers wary and less likely to intrude—and perhaps we've never been able to pinpoint it because we can't establish exactly where each ship or plane disappeared.

This would explain why the United States Navy denies the existence of the Bermuda Triangle and claims that nothing strange has ever occurred there: the navy is in on the deception and covering up the truth.

The Mystery Remains

Are any of these theories correct? Can there possibly be some sort of cover-up about the truth, or does everyone lack the answer or answers?

At this point, it does seem to be anyone's guess as to why the Bermuda Triangle exists and to what really happened to all those boats and planes. New theories are created every day, and perhaps someday one of them will be right.

In the meantime, the Bermuda Triangle remains one of the biggest of unsolved mysteries. Is it a deliberate mystery? If there really is some sort of government cover-up, then the Bermuda Triangle truly is one of the world's strangest secrets.

GLOSSARY

black hole An area of space that has collapsed in on itself, creating a funnel effect; everything in the vicinity is pulled in by the black hole's powerful gravitational field and crushed as it passes through the event horizon.

blockade runner A lightweight ship used for evading a blockage of food supplies or communication by an opposing force in a port or strait, rather than confronting those blocking the passage.

buoyancy The upward force of water that gives it the ability to support heavy objects, allowing them to float.

compass A navigational tool that uses Earth's magnetic poles and a metal pointer to determine what direction a boat or individual is traveling.

compass variation A technique used by navigators to compensate for the difference between magnetic north (on a compass) and true (geographic) north.

current A continuous, directed movement of ocean water generated by heat, wind, gravitational pull, and other forces.

disoriented In a state of confusion, usually of time or place.

extraterrestrial From somewhere outside of Earth's atmosphere.

fabrication An untruthful statement or made-up explanation.

freighter A cargo ship, used for transporting goods.

galleon A large sailing ship distinguished by three to four mizzenmasts, used primarily between the sixteenth and eighteenth centuries for carrying goods or as warships.

illusionist A performer who tricks the members of an audience into believing that they saw something impossible.

magnetic north The direction a compass points; it continually shifts based on the activity of Earth's magnetic fields.

rookie An individual who is relatively new to something.

science fiction A type of fiction that often takes place in the future or an alternate reality where technology is advanced; it relies heavily on established science.

seismic activity The release of energy or movement within Earth's crust.

skeptic An individual who questions beliefs on the basis of scientific understanding.

supernatural Existing outside of explanation or nature.

true north The geographic direction represented on maps and globes by the lines of longitude; the actual direction of the North Pole.

wormhole A miniature black hole, or a theorized tunnel through space and time.

FOR MORE INFORMATION

Bermuda Maritime Museum

P.O. Box MA 133

Sandys MA BX, Bermuda

(441) 234-1333

Web site: http://www.bmm.bm

Housed inside the fortress keep of the old Royal Naval Dockyard, the
museum features six acres of grounds, seven bastions, and eight historic
exhibit buildings holding maritime artifacts.

Hiller Aviation Museum

601 Skyway Road

San Carlos, CA 94070

(650) 654-0200

Web site: http://www.hiller.org

A museum, founded in 1998, with artifacts from the history of aviation.

Historical Museum of Southern Florida

101 West Flagler Street

Miami, FL 33130

(305) 375-1492

Web site: http://www.hmsf.org

A museum dedicated to gathering, organizing, preserving, and celebrating
Miami's history.

Mariners' Museum
100 Museum Drive
Newport News, VA 23606
(757) 596-2222
Web site: http://www.marinersmuseum.org
A museum that showcases over 35,000 maritime items, including some
Christopher Columbus artifacts.

Ohio University Skeptic's Society
Department of Biological Sciences
Ohio University
107 Irvine Hall
Athens, OH 45701
(740) 593-1000
Web site: http://ohiouskepticsociety.blogspot.com
A society of "skeptics" with a goal of promoting healthy skepticism and
science.

The Skeptic's Society
P.O. Box 338
Altadena, CA 91001

(626) 794-3119

Web site: http://www.skeptic.com

A scientific and educational organization of scholars, scientists, historians, magicians, professors and teachers, and anyone curious about controversial ideas, extraordinary claims, revolutionary ideas, and the promotion of science.

Web Sites

Due to the changing nature of Internet links, Rosen Publishing has developed an online list of Web sites related to the subject of this book. This site is updated regularly. Please use this link to access the list:

http://www.rosenlinks.com/me/ber

FOR FURTHER READING

Begg, Paul. Mary Celeste: *The Greatest Mystery of the Sea*. New York, NY: Longman, 2005.

Berlitz, Charles. *The Bermuda Triangle*. Garden City, NY: Doubleday, 1974.

Gaddis, Vincent H. *Invisible Horizons: True Mysteries of the Sea*. Philadelphia, PA: Chilton Books, 1965.

Hicks, Brian. *Ghost Ship: The Mysterious True Story of the* Mary Celeste *and Her Missing Crew*. New York, NY: Random House, 2005.

King, David. *Finding Atlantis: A True Story of Genius, Madness, and an Extraordinary Quest for a Lost World*. New York, NY: Crown, 2006.

MacGregor, Rob, and Bruce Gernon. *The Fog: A Never Before Published Theory of the Bermuda Triangle Phenomenon*. Woodbury, MN: Llewellyn, 2005.

Miller, Connie Colwell. *Bermuda Triangle: The Unsolved Mystery*. Mankato, MN. Coughlan Publishing, 2009.

Moore, William L., and Charles Berlitz. *Philadelphia Experiment: Project Invisibility*. New York, NY: Random House, 1995.

Oxlade, Chris. *The Mystery of the Bermuda Triangle*. Portsmouth, NH: Heinemann, 2006.

Quasar, Gian. *Into the Bermuda Triangle*. New York, NY: McGraw-Hill, 2005.

Rooney, Anne. *Alien Abduction*. New York, NY: Crabtree, 2008.

Stewart, Melissa. *Is the Bermuda Triangle Really a Dangerous Place? And Other Questions About the Ocean*. Minneapolis, MN: Lerner, 2011.

Stone, Adam. *The Bermuda Triangle*. Minneapolis, MN: Bellwether Media, 2010.

Ulanski, Stan L. *The Gulf Stream: Tiny Plankton, Giant Bluefin, and the Amazing Story of the Powerful River in the Atlantic.* Chapel Hill, NC: University of North Carolina Press, 2008.

Vallee, Jacques. *Wonders in the Sky: Unexplained Aerial Objects from Antiquity to Modern Times.* New York, NY: Tarcher, 2010.

Walker, Kathryn, and Brian Innes. *Mysteries of the Bermuda Triangle.* New York, NY: Crabtree, 2008.

West, David, and Mike Lacey (illus). *The Bermuda Triangle: Strange Happenings at Sea.* New York, NY: Rosen Publishing, 2005.

INDEX

About the Authors

Vivian E. Shumway is a Bermuda Triangle enthusiast and author of books for teens. She lives in Michigan.

Aaron Rosenberg is an author of books for teens and lives with his wife and children in New York City.

Photo Credits

Cover, p. 1 (inset image) © www.istockphoto.com/Arne Thaysen; cover, p. 1 (lens) © www.istockphoto.com/jsemeniuk; cover and interior (background image) © www. istockphoto.com/Dominik Dabrowski; p. 5 Newscom; pp. 6, 10, 15, 17, 20, 22, 23, 26, 30, 34, 35, 42, 45, 52 Shutterstock.com; p. 7 © www.istockphoto.com/Nicholas Belton; p. 9 NASA; p. 11 Photos.com/Thinkstock; pp. 13, 18 © Mary Evans Picture Library/The Image Works; p. 24 Darlene Hammond/Archive Photos/Getty Images; p. 27 Apic/Hulton Archive/Getty Images; pp. 28–29 Time & Life Pictures/Getty Images; p. 32 © AP Images; pp. 38–39 Comstock Images/Thinkstock; p. 40 Steve Bronstein/The Image Bank/Getty Images; p. 46 Ray Massey/Stone/Getty Images; p. 48 George Strock/Time & Life Pictures/ Getty Images; pp. 50–51 Hemera/Thinkstock.

Editor: Bethany Bryan; Designer: Matt Cauli; Photo Researcher: Karen Huang